LOOKING BACK AT
Levenshulme & Burnage

Gay Sussex, Peter Helm, Andrew Brown

Willow Publishing 1987
Willow Cottage, 36 Moss Lane,
Timperley, Altrincham,
Cheshire, WA15 6SZ.

ISBN 0 946361 22 3

Printed by The Commercial
Centre Ltd., Clowes Street,
Hollinwood, Oldham.

Contents

Foreword

After completing their book on Rusholme and Fallowfield, which was published in 1984 in the "Looking Back At" series, Gay Sussex and Peter Helm decided to work together on a book about another part of suburban Manchester.

The Levenshulme/Burnage area was an obvious choice. Peter Helm was born in Levenshulme, and his grandparents had farmed the Midway Farm until it was built on in the early years of this century. Gay Sussex had worked at Levenshulme and Burnage libraries, and knew that local people took a strong interest and pride in their area.

A third writer, and inveterate collector of old picture postcards of this area, has joined the team. This is Dr. Andrew Brown of Levenshulme Health Centre, whose collection of over 500 local photographs proved an invaluable source of material for this book.

Looking Back at Levenshulme and Burnage is about our links with the past; its illustrations are often of buildings that have been demolished, or of street scenes that have changed considerably. It is not intended to be a complete history – that would need a much bigger book – but the authors have tried to give a historical review of the area, and to include a wide range of photographs. Hopefully readers will find many that will strike a chord in their memories.

Many people have helped – families, friends, neighbours, library users and Health Centre patients. Institutions and individuals which deserve special mention are the various departments of Manchester Central Library – Local History, Arts, Archives and Photographic; Burnage and Levenshulme libraries, the North Western Regional Library System, North West Sound Archive and the Lancashire Bibliography, the Manchester Studies Unit at Manchester Polytechnic, the City Planning Department, the Portico Library, the Police History Museum, Marks and Spencer plc, members of Rusholme and Fallowfield Civic Society; and Mrs. T. Helm, Mrs. J. Davies, Mrs. M. Millet, Chris Makepeace, the Mattinson family, Mrs. M. McGill, Mr. E. France, Mrs. Moseley, Mrs. J. Wright, Mr. Lowe, and Miss Margaret de la Wyche.

Special thanks to Dorothy Helm and Margaret Baldwin who did the typing and were very helpful. The Brown family and the Sussex family were very patient about all the disturbance involved in producing this book, so thanks to Mavis, Louise and Annemarie Brown, and to Graham, Merida and Jasmine Sussex.

The writers apologise for any errors and hope that they are few. Writing and researching the history of this area has been very satisfying for all three; they hope they have done it justice.

Windsor Road, 1905

An appealing postcard showing the style of children's dress, and curtains, of the time. Mr. and Mrs. Keen showed an understandable pride in their house and pretty daughter, in having this card made to send season's greetings to friends and family.

Introduction

Burnage and Levenshulme make an interesting combination, and many old photographs and postcards are still in existence to show the changes that have occurred over the years. The area has both inner-city busyness and remnants of more rural times, traditional pubs and new restaurants, seedy parts and signs of gentrification, new community centres and village-style neighbourly networks.

The area covered in this book stretches from Crowcroft Park to Fog Lane, with most emphasis around the two main roads, Stockport Road and Burnage Lane. As you read the book, imagine that you are following this route – starting at Crowcroft Park you go along Stockport Road to Crossley Road, then down Crossley Road and back through Cringle Fields to Albert Road. Start again at the corner of Broom Lane and Stockport Road, following Broom Lane to Barlow Road, and then back along Cromwell Grove (and Chapel Street) to Stockport Road and Albert Road. The second part starts at West Point and follows Slade Lane and Burnage Lane as far as Fog Lane and Kingsway.

Hornby's Newsagent, Barlow Road, c.1912 *(left)*

This shop is still with us today, at 61 Barlow Road, but the woman's dress and the newspaper placards place it firmly in Levenshulme's past.

The sale of picture postcards must have been a strong line judging by the Raphael Tuck adverts, and certainly the period 1900–1914 was the peak of their production.

Chapel Street, c.1935

Burdett's Bakery, showing the narrow path through to Mercer Street.

Levenshulme

The boundaries of Levenshulme have traditionally been the Nico Ditch, Pink Bank Lane, Cringle Brook, and Slade Lane/Burnage Lane; and although the authors adopt these boundaries, the book occasionally uses material from over the borders.

Levenshulme's early history is rather vague, largely because the principal landowners lived outside the township, and farmers and yeomen left little documentation. Levenshulme is one of a small group of townships in South Manchester which incorporate the word "Hulme"; they are Hulme itself, Rusholme – "Rush*u*lme" in the mid 19th century – Kirkmanshulme, and Levenshulme, The "hulme" part of these names was pronounced "oom", so that Levenshulme was pronounced "Levenzoom", and the reader may well remember pre-war residents of Hulme speaking of it as "Hoom". In the 19th and early part of the 20th centuries there was little movement of population, and traditional pronunciations continued until, as elsewhere, newcomers arrived, and began to pronounce the name as they found it written. Ekwall says that the name is derived from Leofwine's hulm, Leofwine being a personal name and hulm a Danish word for water meadow, and he quotes a 1246 rendering of the name – Lewyneshulm – to support this view. But it has to be said that there is neither folk-memory nor documentary evidence relating to the existence locally of a Leofwine.

The northern boundary of the township was the Nico Ditch, and, well within living memory, this was visible as a watercourse with a steepish bank on the Longsight side between St. Oswald's Road and Mount Road; in our grandparents' day it would have been open to within 50 yards of Stockport Road. The Ditch ran from Ashton Moss in a south westerly direction until it ended beyond Rusholme at Hough Moss. It was probably built to defend Manchester from attack from the south east by the Danes, and was the most important of a series of these defensive ditches to the east and south east of Manchester. A well-preserved section of the Ditch can still be seen in Platt Fields Park, opposite Old Hall Lane.

The great age of some old ditches and roads can often be told by their use as township boundaries, and both the Nico Ditch and Pink Bank Lane (the old London Road) fall into this category. Both are probably over a thousand years old.

In the Middle Ages there are scarcely any references to Levenshulme. "Lywensholme" was referred to in the survey of Manchester in 1322, when tenants were recorded as "paying their proportion to the maintenance of the bailiffs and under bailiffs of the Manor". Three of the charters of the Collegiate Church (Manchester Cathedral) refer to "Leysholme" (1556), "Lensholme" (1578), and "Lentsholme" (1635). And in the 16th century there are references to the earliest recorded landed proprietors of the township – the Leghs of Baguley. Early in the 18th century, certain lands in the township, owned first by the Leghs, then by John Thorpe of Levenshulme, and finally by Obadiah Hulme of Reddish, were sold to form part of the endowment of Gorton Chapel, being paid for partly by the inhabitants of Gorton, and partly by a grant from the Governors of Queen Anne's Bounty. At the time of the Civil War, John Gilliam Esquire of Levenshulme was a captain in the Parliamentary forces, and it is interesting to speculate that he may have been a friend of Charles Worsley who rose to be a major-general on the same side in the War, and whose father, Ralph Worsley (of Platt Hall, Rusholme) was an important landowner in Levenshulme.

In 1655 there were only 25 persons paying rates. By 1774 there were 56 families living in the township, with a total population of 280. In 1844, when maps and schedules were prepared in connection with tithe redemption, only 1½% of the land was occupied by buildings, another 2½% was ploughed, and all the rest (96%) was meadow and pasture land. The tithes had been payable to the Dean and Canons of the Collegiate Church, which was the parish church of the parish of Manchester, of which Levenshulme was a part.

In 1765, when St. Thomas's church on Wellington Road North, Heaton Chapel was built, a new ecclesiastical parish was created, to include Heaton Norris, Reddish, and Levenshulme; and in 1861, with the population increasing rapidly, St. Thomas's parish was itself divided, the northern part forming a new parish based on St. Peter's church at the corner of Barlow Road (formerly Adlands Lane) and Stockport Road. Early in this century this ecclesiastical parish of Levenshulme was divided into three, and the churches of St. Mark's and St. Andrew's built.

Communications between Levenshulme and the outside world were revolutionised in 1724 by the turnpiking of the main road to Stockport, and 118 years later by the building of the Manchester and Birmingham railway. Prior to 1724, Stockport Road was said to have been nothing more than a lane leading from Manchester via Ardwick Green

Old Cottages, Stockport Road, corner of Longden Road, c.1900

Early 19th century cottages with stone roofs and sliding casement windows. Behind these cottages the road opens out at the junction of Longden Road and Leech Street.

to Longsight and Levenshulme. Under the Turnpike Act, the trustees were given powers to erect tollgates, and to collect tolls for the maintenance of the road, and this resulted for the first time since the Roman era in reasonable road surfaces, which allowed stagecoaches and horse-drawn wagons to move freely in most weather. There was never any need for a tollbar in Levenshulme, as there was no access to the road from other villages between the Longsight tollbar (corner of Slade Lane) and the Heaton Chapel bar (adjacent to St. Thomas's church, Heaton Chapel).

The building of the railway, and the associated industrial revolution, marked the beginning of the end for Levenshulme as a farming community. Easier distribution of manufactured goods increased the demand for them, and the building of more mills and factories in Manchester to meet this increased demand brought tremendous population increases to Manchester, so that, by the end of the 19th century, the farmland of Levenshulme was required for houses to accommodate these increased numbers. Because most of the houses date from the 1880's or later, Levenshulme has escaped the fate of other inner areas, in which there has been wholesale demolition of property and subsequent redevelopment, very often with multi-storey dwellings which have failed to stand the test of time.

As early as 1865, Levenshulme's administration was in the hands of an elected Local Board of Health. Sixteen years later, the Local Board's functions were taken over by one of the new Urban District Councils, and it was the proud boast of the Levenshulme Council that bylaw housing standards were superior to those of nearby areas, and the death rate one of the lowest in the country. In particular, the density of house building was less than elsewhere, and all terraced houses had small front gardens, so that none opened directly on to the street, and all had comparatively large back yards. The U.D.C. had a short life, and, in 1909, Levenshulme was incorporated into Manchester.

The reasons for the development of a small but significant industrial sector in Levenshulme are obscure. For a short time there was a "cotton manufactory" on part of what is now Crowcroft Park, probably before the construction of the Stockport branch of the Ashton canal and its associated mills. Another early sign of industry was the bleach works at Pink Bank Lane. This and the much later Printworks near Mount Road would be making use of the clear water from several brooks flowing through the area. Perhaps the availability of workers proficient in the use of machines and steam power proved to be an attraction to other industries, and by the early 20th century there were groups of works in Manor Road, Chapel Street, and the south end of Stockport Road, providing employment for hundreds of skilled workers.

Changes in demand for the products of Levenshulme's light engineering works together with the continuing trend towards amalgamation and rationalisation (i.e. closing down the less profitable parts of businesses which have amalgamated) resulted in some post-war changes. Perhaps the biggest change arose from the working out of available clay deposits, from which millions of bricks must have been made by Jackson's on their site stretching from the railway (by the tripe works) to the southern end of Cringle Road. Infilling and landscaping have made the site more attractive visually, but it is no longer a source of employment. The tripe works themselves – and their associated shops – have all closed too, as local people seemed to lose their taste for those wonderful products, transferring their loyalties to the Indian and Chinese restaurants, the takeaways, and supermarkets.

Johnson's Map of 1820 *(opposite)*

The immediate impression given by this map is of the sparcity of population. Groups of houses are dotted about, many of them being farm-houses or farm-workers cottages, but hardly anything big enough to be regarded even as a hamlet. Levenshulme is merely a place through which the main North–South road runs. That main road is here Stockport Road, said to have replaced Pink Bank Lane centuries ago as the main road, but still at this time using the old route from Heaton Chapel into Stockport by way of Lancashire Hill. However, there are signs of change: the Stockport branch of the Ashton Canal has been built, and before long the new railway will arrive. Very few of the buildings recorded here can still be seen – Printworks Farm (3) is one – but we show pictures of many which were photographed in their heyday, including Midway House (2), Church Farm (5), the chapel in Chapel Street (7), Black Brook Farm (9), Slade Hill (11), Cringle Cottage (12), Cradock Fold (8), Botany Bay Cottage (6), Hurst Farm (14), and The Bull Inn (15). Talleyrand Lane is the old name for Barlow Road (the section between Levenshulme Library and Pink Bank Lane), and Adlands Lane (opposite Yew Tree Farm) the old name for the Stockport Road end of Barlow Road. Industry is represented only by the Bleach works (10), by the infant Printworks (4) at the left-hand end of the Reservoir, and by the Cotton Manufactory in Crowcroft.

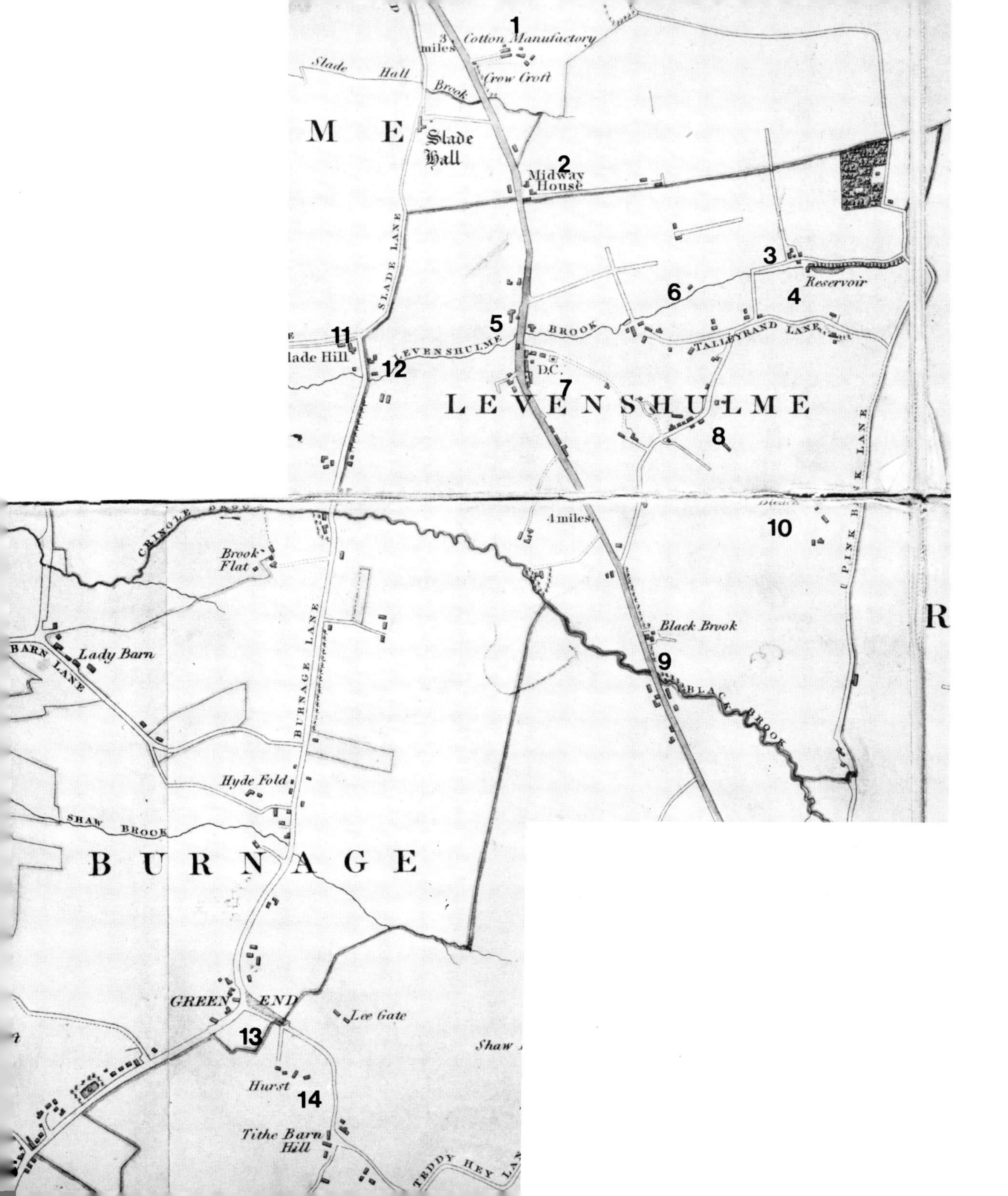

Burnage

Burnage is largely a twentieth century suburb. It lacks the rows of small terraces that sprang up in the 1870's and 1880's in areas such as Levenshulme and Longsight, and lacks also the mansions built nearby by wealthy men in Victorian and earlier eras. Cringle Hall and Burnage Hall were substantial homes, but not stately mansions. Modern housing estates give the area an open and new feel, and the farms are still part of living memory.

The early history of Burnage is somewhat obscure. It had few features of antiquarian note, no nationally important families, no manor, no Roman ruins. Writers tend to rattle on, lyrically but imprecisely, about wild boars, wolves and ancient woods, but deliver few solid facts. The area seems to have grown quietly and sensibly from partly cultivated farmland with two hamlets – Green End and Lane End – to the well-planned and well-maintained suburb it is today.

Sometimes an area's name will give a hint to its origins, but again Burnage is difficult to pin down. Crofton, who was the Clerk of Moss Side Urban District Council and was also an antiquarian historian, gives a hesitant account of how Burnage got its name in an article which appeared in the now defunct Manchester City News in 1908:

> *"Authorities seem to agree that the second syllable represents the word "edge", but as to "burn" they waver between "burn" and "brown". It was possibly land which was at one time peaty moorland, and was brought into cultivation by burning. In 1320 there were some turf peats at the boundary of Heaton Norris and Reddish. At that time, Burnage had its name represented by scribes in the forms Brodage, Bronn-egge, Brown-egge and Bronage. It was also, by some, supposed to take its name from a stream which may have been called the Bourne or Burn, but it is difficult to accept this as the true meaning".*

Ekwall also notes that the etymology is doubtful, and is as guarded as Crofton in his explanation. Although the ground does slope, he felt it improbable that the slope could have been called an edge, certainly it is not in the same league as Alderley Edge. He comments that "burna" might be an old English word for brook, and that perhaps the first part means "brown" and the second part "hedge".

The spelling variations on Burnage complicate this search for the origin of the word. The parish registers of Didsbury which contain the records of baptisms, marriages and burials of many generations of Burnage people give at least sixteen different spellings.

Originally Burnage was part of the sub-manors of Withington and Heaton Norris, and its pastures were farmed by the tenants of these sub-manors. The township gradually developed on the land bordering the old Saltergate, one of the roads along which salt was brought to Manchester from Cheshire. Today, Burnage Lane follows the route of this old road. In 1774 Burnage had 54 houses and 297 residents; in 1851 the population was 563; and in 1901 it was 1,892.

By the turn of the century, Burnage was starting to grow from a village to something approaching a modern suburb, and it was incorporated into Manchester in 1904. However, it still had a number of farms – Tanyard Farm, Dahlia Farm, Hyde Fold Farm, High Farm – and some of the rural charm that Shaw described in 1894:

"It is held to be the prettiest village anywhere near Manchester, still untouched in its cottage existence and rusticity as it is endless in foliage. The lingering life and loveliness are all the more acceptable for the 'progress of growth', devouring space, which is going on around it".

The "progress of growth" as Shaw put it, continued. In 1923 Kingsway opened, its wide modern straight lines providing a contrast to the much older Burnage Lane which, in spite of widening and tree removal, still has something of the country lane about it. Trams commenced running in Slade Lane about 1910, and open-topped solid-tyred buses connected with the Slade Lane terminus and took passengers along Burnage Lane to Northenden. Train travel also opened Burnage up to a wider world when its station opened on 1st May 1909.

Housing schemes also altered the face of rural Burnage. The Burnage Garden Village, a pioneering effort towards the ideal of the garden suburb opened in 1906, and Manchester Corporation developed the Kingsway Housing estate by 1927.

Industrial growth brought some important names to Burnage – Fairey Aviation, Crossley, and Hans Renold. This aspect of the development of Burnage must have given locals some anxious moments. Light industry made Burnage a target for German bombers during World War II. Manchester Local History Library has an Ordnance Survey map, marked in German and used by German pilots, with industrial sites for bombing outlined; Fairey Aviation was one of them. Fortunately the fears of local people were not realised; almost the only bombs to fall on Burnage were those which damaged Burnage High School and nearby houses on the 28th of November, 1940.

Transport, housing and industry tend to swamp farms, country lanes and rural prettiness, but Burnage residents sometimes resisted the onrush of modern Manchester. There was an outcry against the removal of Barcicroft Gate Cottage, once the home of the Watts family, founders of the firm S. and J. Watts, and a protracted campaign against the removal of trees to widen Burnage Lane. Urbanisation is hard to resist however, and today Burnage is a modern suburb with a population of more than 14,000, but it still has a quality of spaciousness and calm, redolent of its days as a village.

This has been a summary of the histories of Levenshulme and Burnage. The following maps and photographs have been chosen to illustrate aspects of their development and character.

Ordnance Survey map, 1908

In the 80 years following Johnson's survey of the area, there was little change in Burnage. In Levenshulme, on the other hand, hundreds of terraced houses had been built on streets newly laid out on either side of Stockport Road and on the south side of Albert Road. The area between Albert Road and the Township boundary (Slade Lane/Nico Ditch) was also fully developed in this period, but with houses of a more substantial nature, often semi-detached and with gardens front and rear, or else – as in Rushford Park – detached and semi-detached houses with long, imposing gardens. By now there were two railways, and a third one projected.

The two completed railways each had a station, and each had substantial sidings to cope with the receipt and despatch of goods, very little of which travelled by road. Industry had blossomed, but was confined to the east and south of the built-up area. Churches, parks, and schools had become established, and although more houses would subsequently be completed, the district was quickly running out of building land.

Crowcroft Park and Midway Hotel area

Crowcroft Hall, Crowcroft Park, c.1920 *(above)*

The house was built about 1840, and from 1889 to 1923 was the rectory for St. Agnes church at the corner of Hamilton Road and Slade Lane. Before Crowcroft Road was made, the road under the railway was Slade Hall Road which would provide the route between church and rectory. When the Styal railway was built, Slade Hall Road was made into a cul-de-sac, and Crowcroft Road was built under a narrower section of the line.

The Unemployed *(below left & right)*

Between the Boer War and the 1914–1918 War, many men were out of work, and Levenshulme suffered with the rest of the nation. As shown in these two photographs, efforts were made by concerned people to alleviate the hardship and organise local unemployed.

In the first photograph a crowd has assembled on Pemberton's estate to listen to a Mr. Grey, one of the organisers. The notice on the gable end of the terrace of houses announces that rents of houses on Pemberton's Crowcroft Park Estate were 5s.6d., 6s.0d., and 7s.0d. a week, but even these amounts would probably have been difficult for the unemployed to find. At this time, there was no system of state benefits although the Council did organise occasional relief work such as street repairs and other public works for which the unemployed received low pay and sometimes a mid-day meal.

The second photograph shows the unemployed camp at Levenshulme, organised by Mr. A. Smith, Captain Williams, and Mr. A. S. Gray (possibly the Mr. Grey of the previous picture). The military influence of Captain Williams is evident – the group "present spades"; and the flag, the tent and the trek cart all give an impression of army life, as it was before the First World War.

Matthews Lane and the Midway

In 1902 the scene at the corner of Stockport Road and Matthews Lane was very different from that at the time of writing. Our first picture shows the land when it was occupied by the original Midway House pub, said to date from 1605.

The Midway House and its extension were both pulled down in 1903, and replaced by a large mock-Tudor pub which still stands. The wooden fence displays a poster announcing a meeting on the 50th anniversary of the Vegetarian Society (founded in 1852), so that the picture must have been taken very shortly before the buildings were pulled down.

In the second picture, taken about 1925 at the corner of Matthews Lane, the Midway House has been replaced by the present Midway Hotel. The end shop on the right was Ogden's the greengrocer. Before incorporation into the City, this area was the boundary between the townships of Rusholme, Gorton, and Levenshulme. All the left-hand side of Stockport Road together with much of the right-hand side was in Rusholme. The pub itself, and Ogden's shop were in Gorton, and the shop with the sunblind was in Levenshulme. The Nico Ditch, which was the township boundary, ran beneath this last shop, and there is a story that on one occasion the floorboards behind the counter gave way, and the shopkeeper fell into the Ditch.

The foreground buildings are still to be seen, but none of the vehicles. Solid tyred charabancs, horse-drawn steel-tyred wagons, and tram cars are only to be seen in museums these days.

The final picture of this group shows Midway Farm house. The telegraph pole is the one seen in the previous picture at the corner of Matthews Lane which means that the present Matthews Lane is built over the site of the farmhouse. The gable end at the right-hand edge of the picture is of Ogden's shop, seen in the previous picture, whilst the more distant houses are those formerly in Fielden Street. The farmland consisted of fields on the left-hand side of Matthews Lane, almost as far as Hemmons Road, and was farmed for the last 25 years or so of its life by Richard Helm, grandfather of one of the authors. Richard's brother farmed the Printworks Farm on Mount Road, and both came from farming stock in the Garstang area of Lancashire.

Midway Farm, Stockport Road at corner of Matthews Lane, pre 1903.

Midway House, Stockport Road, 1902.

Midway Hotel, Stockport Road, c.1925.

Stockport Road and Cringle Fields

Stockport Road, c.1920

Looking south into Levenshulme from the culverted Nico Ditch, this picture shows Stockport Road on a Sunday evening in midsummer. On the right is the wall round the yard of Helm's dairy, and on that wall until the early 1930's, was an enamelled sign with the message *DRIVE SLOWLY THROUGH THE VILLAGE.*

The first street on the right is Park Grove, and behind the shop sign is the tower and spire of the Wesleyan Methodist Church on the corner of Wesley Street (now Woodfold Avenue). The spire was taken down about 1950, but the tower remains. The street on the left, by the telegraph pole, is John Street (now Jean Close), where there was a smithy in the early years of the century. In the 19th century the smithy was 50 yards away in Matthews Lane, and it was there that the massive gates at the Longsight entrance of Belle Vue (sadly destroyed in 1985) were reputedly made. Even the main roads are still gaslit at this date.

Levenshulme Cricket Club, 1904

Levenshulme Cricket Club was on a site occupying the angle of the two railway lines which join at Slade Lane junction, and bounded by Slade Lane and Park Grove. The ground is still there, having been taken over by the Education Department in the 1950's, but the Club and its Carnival have both gone.

Stone Laying, Congregational Church, Stockport Road, c.1905 *(top right)*

The old Sunday School building, between the Church and the end of a terrace of shops, opposite Wesley Street (now Woodfold Avenue), was demolished in two phases. In this picture the rear part of the old building can be seen, and behind it the houses of Thompson Street. In the foreground are the footings of the new building, and a crowd of Congregationalists spilling on to Stockport Road as they take part in the foundation stonelaying ceremony. The Edwardian lady's aversion to the sun is evident from the many parasols which are to be seen.

Levenshulme Mechanics Institution, c.1890 *(right)*

Today the original building can only be recognised at first floor level, as shop fronts have been added to the ground floor. Over the doorway are the words "Levenshulme Mechanics Institution and Schools". At this time the Mechanics Institute movement provided, often, the only source of adult education for the working class.

The picture also shows the old-style, short telegraph pole with only two insulators on each arm. This line of poles was a feature of Manchester's main roads until the mid 1930's.

Stockport Road and Congregational Church, c.1904 *(left)*

On the corner of Mayfield Road (now Mayford Road) is the former Mechanics Institution, and immediately beyond the Church (behind the left-hand end of the tram) is the original Sunday School building which is seen, when partly demolished, in the picture recording the stone laying ceremony of the new building. It is in the early days of the electric trams before the Manchester climate forced the Tramways Department to add upper deck covers.

The three brass balls sign of Oswalds the pawnbrokers can be seen on the left, set against a background of trees at Wesley Street, (now Woodfold Avenue). At this time a trip to the pawnbrokers was a weekly event for some people as they tried to eke out their low pay, or in some cases because they had spent more than was wise on liquor.

The Crescent, Stockport Road, 1914

The Mechanics Institution and Congregational Church are now in the background. In the centre of the picture are the hoardings at the corner of The Crescent and Stockport Road, although nowadays they don't advertise The Rusholme Theatre, or The Grand, or indeed anything local. At the corner of The Crescent is one of the Council's water carts, once a common sight on the road. The three houses in the foreground are in use as shops, the first being a boot maker and repairer, the third "makes clothes, repairs clothes". The shop at the left of the picture advertises Harness Dressing, a necessary product before the arrival of the motor car.

Church Inn, Stockport Road, 1880

In this early picture of the Church Inn, Harrington's the watch repairer's shop on the corner of Yew Tree Avenue had not been built, but both it and the house and shop on the far corner have been demolished in recent years. Levenshulme Terrace is one of three terraces which were built at right angles to the road, and without access for vehicles. The other two – Ethel Terrace near Alma Road, and Rushford Terrace near Slade Lane – have both gone. Down Yew Tree Avenue was the Arcadia. It probably started life as a skating rink, and was converted to a cinema before becoming a wholesale warehouse and then a sports centre. During its time as a skating rink it was host to a memorable Grand Hockey Match, when – as our handbill shows – the Arcadia team played Fred Karno's team, then at the King's Theatre, Longsight. Charlie Chaplin was a member of the Karno's team, and Stan Laurel apparently a non-playing member.

Arcadia Skating Rink
LEVENSHULME.

A GRAND
HOCKEY MATCH
Will be played at the above Rink
On Saturday Afternoon, April 2nd.
BULLY OFF AT 4 P.M.

ARCADIA
VERSUS
Fred Karno's Team
From the Kings Theatre, Longsight.

FRED KARNO'S TEAM:
Goal: Ernie Stone: Full Back: Jimmy Berrisford
Forwards: Fred Jordan, Ted Banks (Capt.), and Charlie Chaplin.
Manager - - Frank O'Niel

Central Avenue, c.1900 *(right)*

Central Avenue is part of Rushford Park, an area of Levenshulme in which medium-sized houses were built closely together, but with long gardens – quite out of character with the rest of Levenshulme. However, the effect is of a quiet leafy suburb, even today. It is linked to Stockport Road by The Crescent, which passes under a railway bridge wide enough to take farm vehicles and machinery, but too low for other vehicles. In 1842, the track under the railway bridge joined the two halves of Yew Tree Farm, but nowadays the section between Central Avenue and the railway is only a footpath. The wooden posts, put in to discourage motor vehicles, survived until the 1930's when they were replaced by the present metal posts. The house showing to the right of the gas lamp was a private school in the 1930's, and is now a private club.

Stockport Road, corner of Barlow Road, c.1919

St. Peter's Church, prominent in this photo, has an interesting history. In 1852 Charles Carill-Worsley of Platt Hall, Rusholme donated 1445 square yards of land and £500 towards the erection of a church in Levenshulme. Being a generous benefactor to churches seems to have been a family trait of the Carill-Worsleys. Thomas Carill-Worsley paid towards the cost of building Holy Trinity Church in Rusholme which was consecrated in 1846. By 1854 St. Peter's School, built at the cost of £1,000 was opened, and this also served as temporary accommodation for the congregation until 1860 when the church itself was consecrated. Carill-Worsley has not been forgotten. In Levenshulme today we have Carill Grove and Worsley Grove just opposite the church.

In this photograph the "Heroes Memorial" in the form of a lych gate, a familiar sight to Levenshulme people, is not yet in position, but the notice board invites donations. It was erected in 1920, and was dedicated and opened by the then Lord Mayor of Manchester, Sir William Kay. In 1949, a panel on the south side of the gate was engraved to commemorate those who died in the 1939–45 war.

Today the church is still as it was but the school closed in 1982, and recently re-opened as the Levenshulme Islamic Centre.

Church Farm, Stockport Road, c.1880 *(right)*

This is a view of the rear of Church Farm on Stockport Road on the site now partly occupied by Barclays (formerly Martins) Bank. At the time when the picture was taken there would be only a field between the farmhouse and the railway line, and the advertisement on the gable end of the wall would be easily readable from the trains.

Church Farm, 54 Stockport Road

George Botham, who was the Levenshulme postmaster in the 1890's, published a Levenshulme directory containing an alphabetic list of the names and addresses of all householders. Very many local businesses advertised in it, including Harry Knibbs of Church Farm, with his primitive view of railway transport.

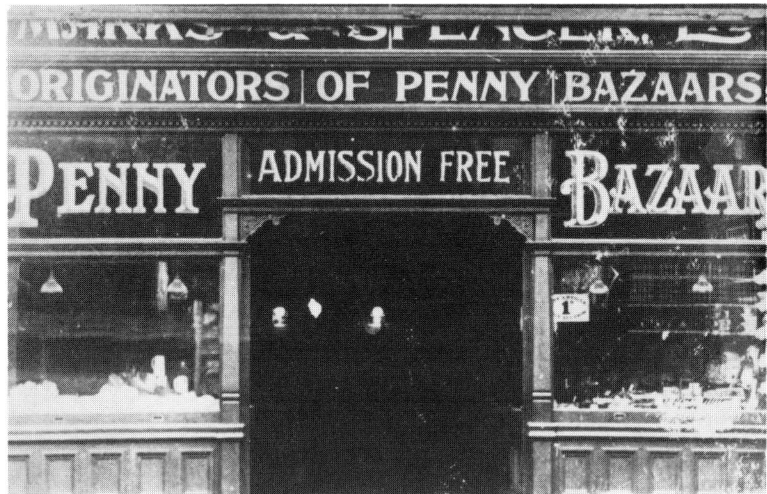

Marks and Spencer's Penny Bazaar, Stockport Road, c.1920

Marks and Spencer's, c.1930.

Marks and Spencer's

From 1915 until 1938 there was a branch of Marks and Spencer's at the corner of Carill Grove East and Stockport Road. For about the first ten years it described itself as a Penny Bazaar, but in its later years – as will be seen from the second picture – it just called itself "Bazaar", even though the local people continued to refer to it as a penny bazaar. In the days when it still called itself a penny bazaar it carried a large notice above the doorway emphasising that a penny was the cost of goods, not the cost of entrance to the shop. The roller shutter, which can be seen partly obscuring the name of the firm in the earlier picture, was a novelty to Levenshulme, but possibly standard practice at the time for Marks.

Railway Inn, corner of Stockport Road and Station View, c.1905 *(left)*

The Railway Inn dates from about 1840, although it was not a pub in its early years, because the 1851 Census shows the Pack Horse as being the only pub in this part of Stockport Road. This house was first of all converted to a pub, and later altered for use as a shop. The front was extended to bring it into line with the adjoining shops, but the Station View elevation was hardly altered.

The Pack Horse, Stockport Road, opposite Farm Yard, c.1890 *(below left)*

A rare picture of this old pub, with the traditional brewer's dray and an early telegraph pole at the left. At the right-hand edge, is the garden wall of the first of a row of old terraced cottages. The mounting block associated with travelling on horse-back is among the barrels to the right of the door. This building was demolished about 1907, and replaced by the present pub.

Gibson's Buildings, next to the Pack Horse, c.1910 *(below)*

These old cottages with their stone roofs and sliding casement windows are similar in style to the early 19th century cottages at Cradock Fold in Broom Lane. They were pulled down to provide a site for the Beswick Co-operative Society's store, and that building is still there, though the Beswick Co-op left it many years ago.

173/175 Stockport Road, c.1890 *(above)*

Two shops as they appeared late last century. They are almost opposite Ethel Terrace and the reflection of Cowan's shop, opposite, can be seen in Wilson's window. The shop blind of McGill's shop is down, and the contents of Wilson's shop window are covered with protective paper, so it must be Sunday. McGill subsequently moved his business to a shop under The Verandah, at Albert Road.

St. Mark's Sunday School *(right)* procession, Stockport Road, 1922

In 1922, the Great War was still very fresh in everyone's memory, and few families would have escaped without loss in the fighting. The wreath at the head of this contingent is probably in remembrance of former Sunday School boys killed in the War. Patriotism was obviously still very much in the air.

The adults in the foreground are Mr. James Fisher, apparitor of St. Mark's, Miss Stubbersfield, in Guide uniform, and Miss Agnes Knowlson, at the right of picture. The Grand Cinema can be seen in the background.

Stockport Road, near Alma Road, 1914 *(right)*

This is the view from Wilson's shop looking towards Stockport. All the houses as far as Alma Park Methodist Church, and the church itself, have now been demolished.

Regal Cinema, Stockport Road, 1959

One of the phenomena of the 1930's and particularly the late 1930's, was the race to build super cinemas, in the belief that here was a form of entertainment which had come to stay. The Apollo, at the Ardwick end of Stockport Road, together with this cinema at the corner of North Western Street were two of them. However, the development of television resulted in the loss of business to the cinemas, and gradually they closed their doors for good, or were converted. The Regal was first of all converted to a ten pin bowling alley, but when bowling alleys turned out to be a nine days wonder, a second conversion took place, this time to bingo; which is how things stand at the time of writing.

Levenshulme Town Hall, c.1905 *(below)*

Levenshulme Town Hall was built in 1898 as the administrative centre of Levenshulme when it was an Urban District Council. Rates were collected and services such as road repair, lighting etc. were organised from this building. Levenshulme was absorbed into Manchester in 1909, and so lost its responsibility for these services. However, the building is still well used. It's a warren of antique stalls known as the Antique Hypermarket, and attracts buyers from all over Manchester.

At the left-hand edge of the picture is part of the one-time Police Station. Over the stone bay can be seen part of the word "Lancaster" and, above that, the rose of Lancashire. When it was built, Levenshulme would be part of Lancashire County, and policed by the County Force.

Council Members, Levenshulme U.D.C.

Members of the Council of the Urban District Council of Levenshulme pose for the camera, possibly at the end of Levenshulme's independent existence.

The Manchester Official Handbook for 1909, the last year of the Urban District Council lists the following councillors:– J. M. McLachlan (Chairman), T. H. Drinkwater, W. H. Winnet, S. Whittall, W. H. Knibbs, R. A. D. Carter, H. S. Smith, F. W. W. Breakell, F. Fenn, R. Burtles, A. Kent, and R. Rostron.

Stockport Road and Broom Lane, c.1907 *(top left)*

Nearly all the buildings seen here remain today. But how the street scene has changed! The tramways had only just changed from horse-drawn trams, and transport relied almost entirely on the horse, using steel-tyred wagons of the type seen here. The wagons standing outside The Wheatsheaf are probably loaded with cotton waste from the mills along the Stockport branch of the Ashton canal.

Dobson's Dairies, Lloyd Road, 1945

Nearly all milk was delivered by horse and cart or on foot before 1939, but after the War there were big changes, and within a very short time electrically-driven vehicles similar to the one shown here had taken over almost completely from the horse. Dobson's was the biggest dairy in Levenshulme before the 1939 War, although Drabble's had a pasteurising plant in Carill Grove East. Eventually all the Levenshulme dairies came under the umbrella of Northern Dairies, a company which in Levenshulme is still based on the Dobson's buildings in Lloyd Road.

Black Brook Farm, Wellington Road North, c.1900 *(right)*

The buildings in this picture are of Black Brook Farm, so called from the Black – or Cringle – Brook which ran through its fields. This farm once occupied the land opposite McVitie's biscuit works. In the foreground is the gate and cart track leading to High Farm; that cart track is now Crossley Road. The man in the picture is presumably going to carry on mending the wall after his break. Tradition says that the small area beyond the wall was used for breaking stone for use in repairing the main road.

Wellington Road, near Belmont Bridge, Heaton Norris, 1903 *(left)*

This is one of the last horse trams – if not the very last – to run between Manchester and Stockport. The tram standard supporting the new conductor wires can be seen in front of the left-hand corner of the house, so that everything is ready for the changeover to electric trams. The tram shown here is one of the Eades patent single-ended cars in which the saloon pivoted on the truck, and could be turned at the end of the journey while the truck remained stationary on the track. The fleet number of this car (L110) indicates that it is based at one of the Longsight depots, and the board across the saloon windows says "Piccadilly Longsight Levenshulme". The later electric trams ran until 1949 when the last examples were replaced by diesel-engined buses.

Crossley Road, c.1880 *(below)*

Crossley Road (or High Lane or Cow Lane, as it was then), looking back across the railway towards Stockport Road, showing the roofs of houses on Stockport Road. In the foreground is a traditional gipsy caravan. The track is here still gated, the white gate posts being visible near the bridge.

Fairey Engineering Works, Crossley Road, c.1929 *(below right)*

The imposing front entrance to the Crossley Works on Crossley Road is seen here. Production of Crossley cars had ceased by 1930, though buses continued to be made (at Gorton) until about 1948. The car manufacturing side of the business passed to Willys Overland Crossley Ltd., and Willys and Overland cars were made until the outbreak of war in 1939. The mascots on top of the Company sign board represent the Willys Knight (a rather shadowy symbol in this picture) and the Overland Whippet cars. The former was an executive-type car, and the latter a popular car, with fingertip throttle control from the top of the steering column. The Whippet's performance was outstanding at the time – "perfect hill climbing, quick off the mark, and petrol consumption of roughly 40 mpg".

Fairey Engineering Works, Crossley Road, c.1928 *(above left)*

Willys Overland Crossley fitting shop. The assembly line technique adopted here was one of the first in the North of England. The small car in the left-hand line is the Overland Whippet in the early stages of assembly. The complete car sold for £125 in 1927/1929. On the right-hand line is the bodywork for the then famous 25 cwt van.

Fairey Engineering Works, Crossley Road, c.1940 *(above right)*

Part of the production line of the Fairey Battle light bomber, used in the early days of the 1939–1945 War. King George VI is here seen inspecting the production line, and – more importantly during the War – being seen by the workers. The King is accompanied by Sir Richard Fairey and Major T. M. Barlow, together with government ministers, designers, and security staff. It is said that the King stopped to ask a workman "What do *you* make?", to which the man, undeterred by the royal presence, is reputed to have replied "Time and a half, Your Majesty".

Cringle Fields area

Before the 1914–1918 War, nearly all of Burnage to the east of Burnage Lane was an unbroken tract of agricultural land, farmed from High Farm (on what is now Crossley Road) or from Dahlia Farm on Burnage Lane. But in the early 1920's, when Manchester Corporation was building houses at a tremendous rate, this area was high on the list for such development. A sketch plan of 1926 shows the whole area from Ranford Road to Shawbrook allocated either as a housing estate or as a public park. At that time, Errwood Road was under construction; with Shawbrook Road, Avon Road, and Crossley Road all finishing at the City boundary, which runs through Cringle Fields. Subsequently, Crossley Road was the only one to be extended to Stockport Road. Another change of plan was to use the site of High Farm house and the large field adjoining it for the building of Levenshulme High School for Girls.

Crossley Road, c.1925 *(above right)*

This view shows the newly-built Crossley Road. On the right can be seen High Farm which was demolished when Levenshulme High School was built on the field at the right of the picture. On the left, the small cottage with the tree in front had a duck pond behind it. As the pond could not be built over, the houses which were subsequently built on Crossley Road had to be set back. Behind the small cottage can be seen Hawthorn Drive, probably in the process of being built. The first forty houses in Hawthorn Drive, Redthorn Avenue, and Whitethorn Avenue were built for the Manchester and Salford Co-operative Society, reputedly for the managers of their shops. Many have now been sold. The marks on the road are typical of those made by horse-drawn carts with steel-tyred wheels.

Cringle Brook and Cringle Fields, c.1900 *(right)*

Before Errwood Road was built, and these fields became a public park, this bridge (at bottom right) across the Cringle Brook was the junction of two footpaths. Through the trees, and off the bottom right-hand corner of the picture can be seen the main path which followed the brook as it meandered from Levenshulme to Burnage. In the foreground, and out of the picture (bottom left) is the footpath leading to Errwood Crescent. A branch out of the main footpath crossed a footbridge – not visible in this picture – leading to the Catholic Church on Clare Road. The footpath to Levenshulme followed the line of trees off the middle right of the picture, under the railway, and out to Stockport Road almost opposite to Lloyd Road.

The footpath under the railway must pre-date 1842, as a special bridge was built to carry the line over it, and that bridge can still be seen a few yards south of the point where Cringle Brook flows beneath the railway.

Cringle Brook, looking towards Burnage, c.1900 *(right)*

A late summer view of Cringle Brook and the footpath to Burnage, showing Burnage House among the trees. This picture is taken from a point near to the present-day junction of Ranford Road and Kempton Road. The brook seen in the picture still forms the boundary between the gardens of Ranford Road and Milwain Road. The path in the picture continued until it reached Burnage Lane opposite Cringle Hall. The cereal crop waiting to be gathered in would probably belong to High Farm on what is now Crossley Road.

Cringle Fields Bandstand, c.1929

In the early years of Cringle Fields the bandstand enclosure was used for worship by the congregations of local churches which had taken part in the annual Whit Week procession of Witness. Each sector of the seating was reserved for a named church, the white panel on the left of the bandstand reading "Stockport Road Congregational". The banner of the "Cong" can be seen above the line of people filing into the seats. Behind the crowds are the roofs of the "new" houses in Woodland Road. The lady in black near the bandstand is Mrs. Bowler, from Highfield Farm, and the bandstand is one of the few remaining in Manchester parks.

St. Mary's Church & Schools, Clare Road, c.1910 *(right)*

These buildings are, from left to right, the Convent of Poor Clares, the Church of St. Mary of the Angels and St. Clare, and the School. A church was built here in 1853 but replaced by a new building in 1879. This photograph will be of the one built in 1879. The Convent was opened in 1869, and the school building came last of all. In 1957 the church closed, and the congregation transferred to a "new" church – the converted Grand cinema on Stockport Road opposite Alma Road. Later still, a new church was built in Elbow Street, and the former cinema reverted to secular use, as an antique dealer's business. The old church building on Clare Road has been converted to provide additional facilities for the school.

Broom Lane, Barlow Road and Chapel Street

Broom Lane, near to Stockport Road, c.1910 *(left)*

How narrow Broom Lane was when the small cottages at the left were still there! They dated from about 1840, and were pulled down many years ago to widen the road, although even today it is still quite narrow for the amount of traffic which uses it. The stepped pavement on the left is still to be seen.

Cradock Fold, Broom Lane, c.1970

This group of old houses just off Broom Lane was associated with a handful of small farms along the lane. The stone roofs and sliding casement windows of some of these houses put their building date very early in the 19th century.

Cradock Fold Cottages, corner of Broom Lane and Highfield Road, c.1900 *(below)*

The picture may have been taken as demolition commenced, although the presence of a family group at the gate perhaps indicates that the nearer part of the building is being altered and re-roofed.

Foundation stonelaying, St. Mark's Church, September 14th 1907 *(below right)*

The ceremony of laying the foundation stone of the new St. Mark's church was a freemasons' occasion. The Earl of Lathom – a provincial grand master – was accompanied in procession from Levenshulme Town Hall by civic dignitaries, church officers, the Levenshulme Prize Band, and 400 masons in full regalia, some of whom are in the foreground of the picture. Keeping an eye on the proceedings, in the background, are Richard Helm and his milk boy Freddy Atkins, who are standing on the roof of the shed at the end of the yard of their dairy on the corner of Barlow Road and Molyneux Road.

Kendrick's shop, corner of St. Mark's Street and Barlow Road, 1922 *(below)*

This picture postcard was sent to Mrs. Coombs in Swansea. A Coombs family lived at a house on the right-hand side of Barlow Road, indicated by the shadow near the edge of the picture, and the card would probably be sent from there. Before the arrival of the telephone, lengthy messages were sent by letter, shorter ones by postcard. The development of the photogravure printing process resulted in the production of picture postcards, and these soon caught the imagination of the public, so much so that the sending and collecting of picture postcards became all the rage for about 20 years. These postcards are now a valuable historical source, representing as they do the local scene as it was 60 to 80 years ago.

St. Mark's Rectory, Barlow Road, c.1905 *(right)*

St. Mark's rectory stood at the corner of Printworks Lane and Barlow Road, on the site now occupied by a garage. In the late 1930's the rectory was replaced by a new building on Mount Road opposite Greenbank Fields, but the old rectory continued to be used for residential purposes for a further 25 years or so, before being pulled down. In this picture the first rector, the Rev. J. Wood, is seen at the garden gate. He was rector from 1902 to 1915, using the school building at the corner of St. Mark's Street as his church until the present church was completed in 1908.

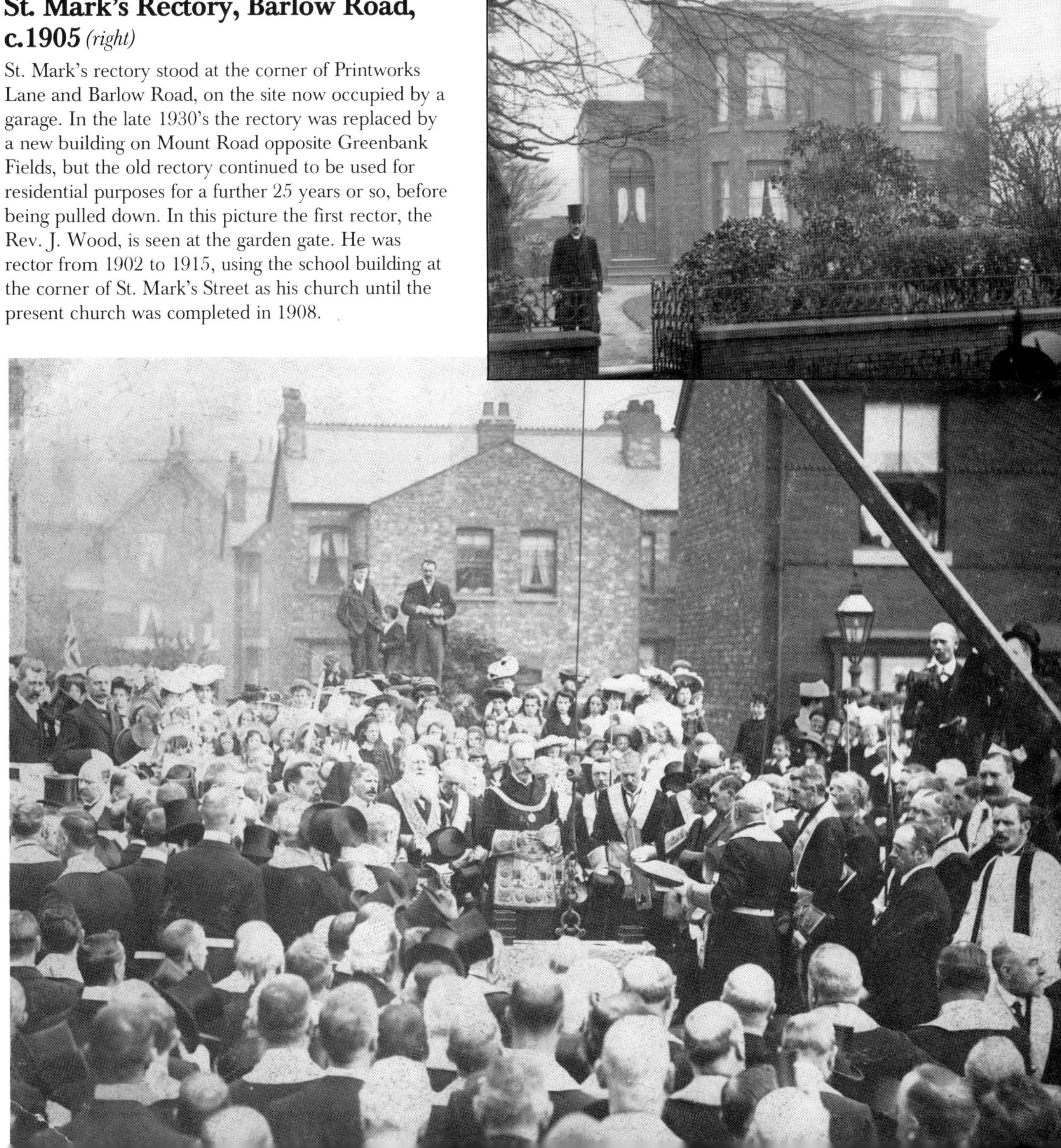

Printworks Farm, c.1883.

Printworks Farm, Mount Road

During the 1860's, three brothers migrated to Levenshulme from their father's farm near Calder Vale north-east of Garstang. The eldest of the three became the "farm bailiff manager" (1871 Census description) at Printworks Farm, whilst the second became a "provision dealer and cowkeeper" (1871 Census) at Veronica Terrace, Stockport Road, almost opposite what is now Woodfold Avenue, and had moved to the 33 acre Midway Farm before the end of the decade. The youngest brother, John, was also living at Printworks Farm in 1871, his occupation being shown as "warehouseman calico printer". He had been picked out by the management of the nearby printworks as an intelligent youth, and went into their employment, eventually – it is said – rising to become a director of the C.P.A., and moving house by stages through Stockport to Wilmslow.

The first of the three pictures shows the scene in the farmyard of Printworks Farm about 1890, with Thomas Helm – eldest of these three brothers – and the family. The farmhouse still stands on Mount Road, and even the outbuildings on the right are still there (1987), behind the petrol filling station which now occupies the foreground of the picture. The second picture shows the second string to Thomas's bow – he was a dealer in horses, though only in a small way. In the third picture, Thomas's son Richard, and Richard's wife Henrietta, are seen in the trap which they often used for travelling to see relatives as far away as Preston. When the farmlands were taken over for building and recreational uses, Dick set up in business as a dairyman at the corner of Barlow Road and Molyneux Road (see picture of stone-laying ceremony at St. Mark's Church).

Thomas Helm (and client?), by the duck pond behind Printworks Farm, c.1900.

Richard and Henrietta Helm, c.1910.

Byrom House c.1900.

Byrom House c.1890.

Byrom House, Barlow Road, c.1900

Protected from the public gaze by the high garden wall on Barlow Road and by the luxuriant vegetation, Mrs. Gyte and her companions take tea. A hammock is slung behind the maid, and perhaps another one has been taken down to allow the photograph to be taken, whilst a birdcage is suspended from the tree just to the right of the door. Obviously a warm summer's day although the dress of the ladies makes no concession to the weather.

Byrom House, Barlow Road c.1890

Another view of the garden of Byrom House when the vegetation was less rampant. Old Mr. Gyte is on the left.

Barlow Road, corner of Broom Lane, c.1906 *(right)*

The section of Barlow Road from here to Pink Bank Lane (Nelstrop Road) was known as Talleyrand Lane, believed to be named after the famous French diplomat Charles Maurice de Talleyrand. On the left is the garden wall of Byrom House; the nearer part of this wall was demolished to allow the building of Byrom Avenue and part of Byrom Parade shops. In the distance is the ridge of St. Mark's School, used as a church before the present church was built. The new church was built on waste land, here seen in the middle distance, fenced off to protect the site as building operations commenced. An unusual feature is the cast metal street nameplate suspended from the arm of the lamp post.

Byrom Parade, Barlow Road, c.1913

The policeman with his white gloves awaits the convoy of cars carrying King George V. The second shop is "closed all day" on the occasion of the King's visit, but Chadwick's – with Mr. Chadwick in the door, standing near to adverts for Hudson's soap and Panshine – and the Byrom Fruit and Potato Stores are open. The wicker baskets outside the greengrocer's shop were still made for general use although their days were numbered. At the left of the picture, the farmhouse of Wolfenden's farm was still standing, where Greenbank Fields are now.

Greenbank Fields *(below left & right)*

Wolfenden's Farm house stood close to the present entrance to Greenbank Fields at the end of Byrom Parade. In common with most of the local farms the Wolfendens were primarily dairy farmers, but it is rare to find a picture of Levenshulme on which cattle are to be seen. The track across the middle of the picture ran from Barlow Road – just off the right of the picture – to join another track from the Printworks to the junction of Cromwell Grove and Barlow Road. At the junction of the two tracks, in the middle of what are now Greenbank Playing Fields, was Botany Bay Cottage, the name of the "pretty cottage" in the picture. The houses to the left are those in Rowsley Avenue.

Botany Bay Cottage, c.1910.

Greenbank Farm (Wolfenden's), Barlow Road, c.1900.

The Old Blue Bell Inn, Barlow Road, c.1910 *(below)*

The old Blue Bell stood on a site adjacent to the present pub, and had been there in one form or another, it is said, for 700 years. Certainly the cruck form of the roof timbers of an earlier building which has been incorporated into the one seen here, appears to confirm its age. Over the years it had accumulated legends, including one that Dick Turpin was a regular caller. The terrace of houses on Lincoln Avenue, at the left of the picture, are here still being built.

Levenshulme Library, Cromwell Grove, c.1910 *(above)*

Levenshulme Library, opened in 1903, still looks much the same today except that poplar trees now hide much of its Edwardian charm and the street light has gone. This library was a "Carnegie" library, a beneficiary of the generosity of Andrew Carnegie the industrialist, whose personal philosophy was to give money back to the people through grants. Some Levenshulme residents expressed doubts about the morality of the Urban District Council accepting this money, as it was thought to be "tainted" because of Carnegie's suppression of trade unions in the United States. But tainted or not, the library was built, and today it is part of what makes Levenshulme a pleasant place to live in.

The Primitive Methodist (Tin) Chapel, Cromwell Grove and Mercer Street, c.1918 *(below)*

This photograph is of the wedding party at the marriage of Mr. and Mrs. Holt. The authors do not know the names of guests except for the lady in dark clothes at the right-hand end of the front row. She is Mrs. Wakefield, whose son Bob married Nellie Helm, the daughter of Dick and Hetty, originally from the Printworks Farm. After its closure the chapel was a film studio for a time, and was demolished after the Second World War.

Cromwell Cottage, Cromwell Grove, c.1910 *(below right)*

These photographs show two views of Cromwell Cottage near the corner of Stockport Road and Cromwell Grove just behind the shop which for many years was occupied by Estelle Modes. They give an idea of family life as enjoyed by the more comfortably off Edwardians of Levenshulme.

The pitch of the roof and the mouldings round the windows date the cottage to about 1840. The crenellated wall survived until the 1960's, long after the building itself had gone.

In the second photograph the Drinkwater family pose for the photographer in front of the summer house in their garden. Councillor Drinkwater of the Levenshulme Urban District council is the bearded member of the group. The Drinkwaters were related to the Mattinsons of Byrom House.

In the garden of Cromwell Cottage.

Cromwell Cottage

Levenshulme Brook, c.1900 *(left)*

Levenshulme Brook – otherwise known as Fallowfield Brook – entered Levenshulme at Highfield Farm on Pink Bank Lane (Nelstrop Road) where, in the 19th and early 20th centuries, it had been dammed to supply the Bleach Works. It crossed Broom Lane where Essex Street (Elmsworth Avenue) is today and crossed Chapel Street at Ratcliffe Street. At this time the area was open fields, the only buildings being in or close to Stockport Road. In this picture the brook is near Stockport Road. St. Peter's Church can be seen at the top right. The gable ends are of the houses on either side of Cromwell Grove.

Chapel Street Schools, 1917 *(right)*

These children and teachers are from the Tin School – the corrugated steel building between the Library and main school buildings, which served as an extension of the school. Miss Robertson (on left) was headmistress of the Tin School, and Miss Ashton (on right) the teacher of this class. Houses in Ratcliffe Street form the backdrop. Among the faces which have been recognised on the back row are Noel Stanworth (5th from left), Edna Porter (8th from left), and Lilian Worrall (10th from left). Chapel Street Schools were opened in 1903.

Wesleyan Chapel, Chapel Street, looking towards Stockport Road, c.1960 *(right)*

This was the first dissenting chapel to be built in Levenshulme, and dates from 1797, about two years before the architecturally very similar Platt Chapel was built on Wilmslow Road. It was closed in 1866 when a new Wesleyan Methodist Church was built at the corner of Woodfold Avenue and Stockport Road on land which had been part of Yew Tree Farm. The old chapel continued to be used for some years as a Sunday School and it was said that the Christmas parties given here in the 1880's were the best in Levenshulme.

The Chapel is the building with three tall windows and a doorway, just to the left of the pedestrian.

Postcard views

The date must be around 1907. St. Peter's still has its ivy, and the lych gate is not yet erected; and those boater-hatted gentlemen on the bowling green look pre-World War I. The Wesleyan Mission Hall on the corner of Ratcliffe Street and Chapel Street was demolished in 1985.

Albert Road, Marshall Road corner, c.1910 *(right)*

The imposing building with the yellow brick front is the old Crown Post Office which was replaced in the 1930's by the present Post Office. The old building was subsequently occupied by the Chapelmoor stationery business, and the crest and balustrade were removed about 1983 when they became unsafe.

The railway embankment at Levenshulme station is in the background. Until 1979 when the new Levenshulme Health Centre was opened the building beyond the old Post Office had been a doctor's home and consulting rooms for more than 50 years. The last doctors to have a surgery in this building were Doctors Andrew and Arthur Brown.

West Point and Slade Lane

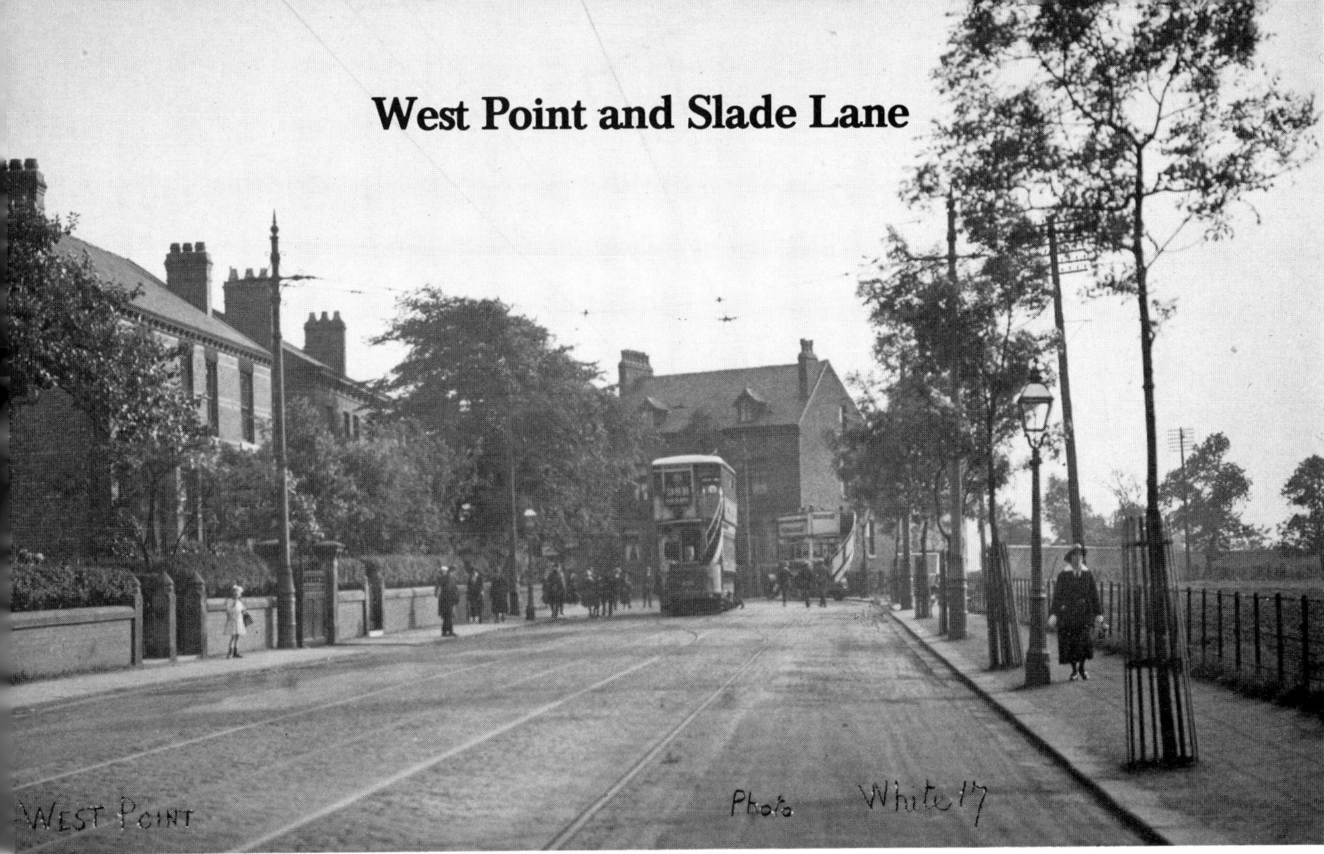

West Point looking from the top of Victoria Road towards Slade Lane, c.1910.

West Point, looking towards Longsight, c.1910.

West Point looking from the top of Slade Lane towards Victoria Road, c.1925.

West Point

At the beginning of the 20th century the whole of Burnage Lane/Slade Lane was a winding narrow country lane, and the tram terminus was only a few yards along from Stockport Road. About 1910, and just before the semi-detached houses between Old Hall Lane and West Point were built, the lane was widened and re-aligned. Ten years later the road at West Point was again widened to make it compatible with the width of the new road (Kingsway) which was about to be driven through to East Didsbury. At this time the electric tramcar was still the principal source of public transport. Motor buses were in the early stages of evolution, and provided feeder services between outlying areas and the nearest tram terminus.

Our earliest picture is of Slade Lane at West Point after its initial widening, but before the shelter was built on the right-hand side. The tram is about to return to Hyde Road Depot, whilst the open-topped, solid-tyred Corporation bus beyond it will soon be on its way along Slade Lane and Burnage Lane to Northenden. The house beyond these two vehicles was pulled down to allow Kingsway to be built. Leaving the right of the picture is the track to Slade Farm, the site of which is now occupied by the houses at the cul-de-sac end of Kingsmere Avenue.

A slightly later picture shows the same scene, but from the Burnage end of West Point. The new houses are those in Lytham Road, and by this time the tram shelter has been built. The bus has a characteristically tram-shaped body. Later still, in the third picture, the road has been further widened so that the tram shelter is now on an island. Before trams started running along Kingsway the tracks were realigned, with a new central island between the south and north bound tracks. The house just to the left of the open-topped bus is Hawthorn Cottage built about 1840 for Samuel Roylance de la Wyche who owned Yew Tree Farm, the farmhouse of which was in Yew Tree Avenue. Almost 150 years later, Hawthorn Cottage is still occupied by the family firm.

Slade House, Slade Lane, opposite Osborne Road, c.1909 *(above)*

At this date Kingsway had not been built; the two houses at the far right of the picture had to be demolished to make way for that new road some 15 years later. The grounds of Slade House were extensive, stretching from Slade Farm buildings as far as Monica Grove on Burnage Lane, so that both Albert Road extension – between Slade Lane and the newly-built Kingsway – and Kingsway itself had to be cut through the grounds. The gateway at the back of the house may still be seen in Green Drive, and is now in use as the entrance to Moseley Court.

Kingsway Super Cinema *(above right)*

This cinema, with its obligatory verandah on the left to shelter the queuing crowds, was built in 1929. In the early 1950's, when the network of tramlines was no longer in use, the present roundabout was built. The cinema was demolished in the 1970's and replaced by Apex House. Locals have claimed that the Kingsway Cinema was famous only for the number of times that the film used to break!

Slade Lane Garage, 1932 *(right)*

This odd-looking building appears to have been purpose-built as a garage, and has changed only by the addition of a front-office block built on to the white-washed wall. When the photograph was taken the office was in a wooden lean-to at the left-hand side. The Redline petrol pump is just to the left of the main doorway, and is twice the height of the man standing there. Motor oil was dispensed "loose" from the two cabinets between the doorway and the car. On the wall is a sign saying "Accumulator charging depot" a facility needed by the many people without an electricity supply. Their "wireless sets" were powered by a 120 volt dry battery, and by a small lead-acid battery (or accumulator) which required re-charging once or twice a week.

Grange Avenue, from Slade Lane, c.1900

Grange Avenue was laid out about 1880, and the photograph shows some of the earliest buildings. They are two pairs of large semis, the first pair being called "The Limes", and the second one "The Beeches". At that time there were no houses on the island site between the two arms of Grange Avenue. In the distance can be seen the terrace of houses in Birch Grove off Forest Range. According to Miss E. Watts Sidebottom, the trees on Grange Avenue were planted by Mr. Samuel Watts, of S. & J. Watts, who lived at Burnage Hall.

The Field Path, Levenshulme (now the entry behind Scarisbrick Road houses), before 1906

Before Kingsway and the two railways were built, the path in this photograph ran along the edge of the fields from Slade Lane to Small Oak Farm which stood where the corner of Brailsford Road and Braemar Road is now, through Small Oak and Large Oak farmyards, and on to Ladybarn Road and Fallowfield village.

The Thirlmere aqueduct, which follows the old L.N.E.R. railway line from the Stretford boundary to the Reddish boundary, had to be diverted in Fallowfield and Levenshulme to avoid disturbance to buildings. It is buried under this footpath (now the entry) and continues via Grange Avenue, Alexandra (now Arliss) Avenue, Alma Park Schools, York Street, Stockport Road, Crayfield Road and Broom Lane, until it returns to the railway near the old tripe works.

The house in the centre of the picture is Danebury (originally Ramsey Lodge), and it is still there today on the corner of Grange Avenue and Slade Lane. The date must be before 1906 as the Scarisbrick Road houses have not yet been built.

Slade Lane, Levenshulme, near former Duchess of York Babies Hospital, c.1900 *(below)*

This picture is of the Burnage end of Slade Lane, the boundary being formed by the Cringle Brook which flows under the road near the distant bend. The bridge and road have not yet been widened. On the left is Cringle Brook Cottage where Linden Park (formerly Linden Road) is now. Northbrook House, until 1986 the Nurses Home of the Hospital, is at the right-hand edge. The gateway in the bottom right-hand corner opened on to a track along the railway boundary, giving access to the fields between Northbrook House and the Styal railway line. It is now the entrance for Rodney House and playing fields.

Slade Lane (Burnage end), c.1905 *(right)*

A view from the position of Cringle Hall Road, looking back towards West Point, with the railway bridge beyond the horse-drawn trap. Cringle Brook Cottage just shows between the lamp post and trees, with Northbrook House on the left. The children on the left are in the southern gateway to Northbrook House, and the open doorway near the left-hand edge is the pedestrians' entrance to Cringle Hall.

Cringle Hall (former Duchess of York Hospital), c.1920 *(right)*

An interesting picture, taken at visiting time, of the cots at the Babies' Hospital, moved outside for fresh air treatment. At that time it was believed that fresh air was beneficial to the sick. Note at the left, the very small cots for the tiny babies, and behind them a ward, converted from the typical Victorian conservatory of the Hall.

Cringle Hall formed the nucleus of the Babies' Hospital (until 1986 the Duchess of York Hospital), although little of the original building remains. In 1951, it was found to be structurally unsound, and the upper floors were demolished.

The Babies' Hospital took over Cringle Hall in 1919, after several years during which the Hall had been used partly as a military hospital and partly as a private residence.

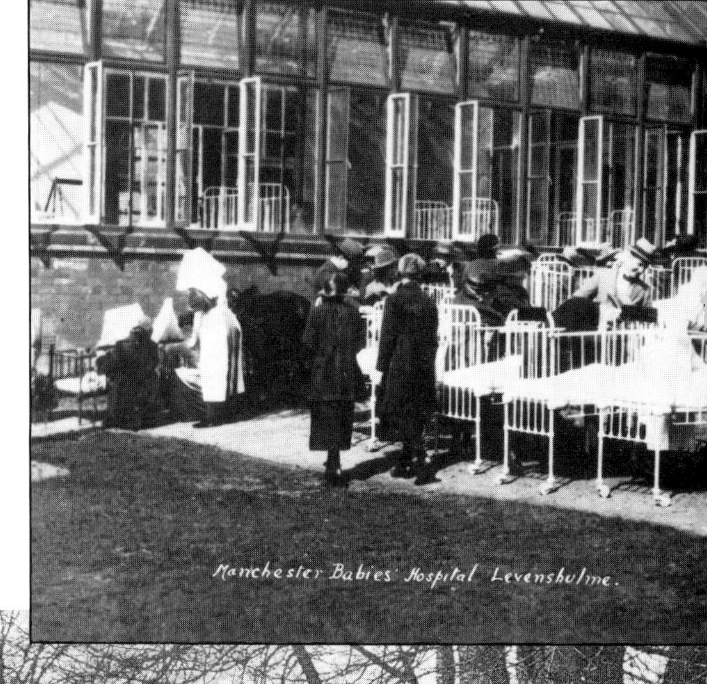

Burnage

Drawing by S. B. Corbet.

Burnage Lane, looking towards Cringle Hall, 1916 *(left)*

The house on the left is Burnage Lodge, which has since been pulled down and replaced by Burnage Court flats. Immediately beyond the privet hedge is an opening which was the entrance to Burnage Hall kitchen area and outbuildings, and by this time had been converted into an entry for the houses in Burnage Hall Road. The boy posing in the foreground, in charge of the traditional confectioner's cart, works for "E. Smith & Sons, Confectioners"; and the wall on the right protects the garden of Brook House (until 1986 the Duchess of York Hospital outpatients' building) from the public gaze.

Burnage Hall, c.1900 *(below left)*

Burnage Hall, built around 1840, was a substantial brick and stone house with ornamental gardens, orchards and glasshouses, set back about 150 yards from Burnage Lane and approached by a magnificent avenue of lime trees some of which can still be seen in Burnage Lane.

Samuel Watts moved into the Hall about 1846. He was one of the sons of John Watts, founder of the firm S. & J. Watts which built a palatial warehouse in Portland Street, Manchester, now the Britannia Hotel. The other son, Sir James Watts, lived at Abney Hall, Cheadle.

Miss E. Watts Sidebottom writes that the clay dug to make the bricks to build Burnage Hall came from a field where the Garden Village now stands. The resulting hollow formed a pond "and it was for some years used for curling matches, and great was the excitement and the shouting, and many were the cabs, four-wheelers, and hansoms, which drove up on a clear winter's day. At night fires were lit and the game continued with no lessening of enthusiasm until late at night". The Hall and grounds (about 36 acres) fetched £14,000 at auction, and the house was demolished in 1911 to allow the building of Burnage Park Estate. The outbuildings remained and were used by Bidder's the scaffolding firm, until subsequent demolition when two houses were built on the site.

Burnage Lane, corner of Grangethorpe Drive, 1911 *(left)*

New houses in Grangethorpe Drive are here being offered for sale. The fencing and gates originally gave access to a house about 50 yards from the road, but appear to have been retained when the new "high-class semi-detached villas" were built, as the road is still gated on the 1923 maps.

The sign for Grangethorpe Drive Estate advertises the estate agent (and probably the builder) as T. Turnbull, who also built many houses in Levenshulme, including those on Broom Avenue, and the roads off Broom Avenue, which have "T.T." name plaques on them. There are also similar plaques on Stockport Road opposite Clare Road and in Longsight.

Burnage Miniature Railway, Moorton Avenue, c.1910 *(below left)*

This miniature railway ran in the garden of Moorton Lodge at the cul-de-sac end of Moorton Avenue from approximately 1910 to 1930. It was operated by a Mr. T. Foster who built the track and signal box etc. in his garden and was in the habit of giving rides to local children at weekends. Beyond the fence were the open fields of High Farm (Crossley Road) and Dahlia Farm (Burnage Lane) on which the Corporation housing estate was later built.

(opposite, top)

Entrance, Garden Village, c.1912

This picture shows the Garden Village almost completed. Main Avenue is still very narrow, with fences in a decorative rustic style typical of the period.

The Edwardian reformers' ideal of "The Garden Suburb" was of well-designed houses which the ordinary wage-earner could afford to rent, set in their own gardens, and with plenty of communal space for recreation to encourage the development of a real community spirit.

Burnage Garden Village was part of this movement. In Manchester a number of organisations supported it, including the Manchester Statistical Society, the Manchester Society of Architects, and the Manchester and Salford Sanitary Association. T. C. Horsfall (of Ancoats Hall) and T. R. Marr, who were social reformers of the early 1900's, were at the forefront of the movement, and in 1902 they founded the Citizens' Association for the Improvement of the Unwholesome Dwellings and Surroundings of the People.

A public meeting was held in the C.W.S. committee rooms in Balloon Street on the 26th June 1906 at which Manchester Tenants Limited was formed to establish a garden suburb. Capital was raised with the issue of shares and loan stock, each tenant being required to hold at least two £10 shares. A plan was adopted which would "provide that each house should be placed so as to have the maximum amount of light and air and pleasantness of outlook and also to secure some open space for recreation". The houses were mostly semi-detached and had bathrooms, hot and cold running water and electric lighting. Facilities included a bowling green, tennis courts, and space for allotments and children's playground. Later a village hall was built and the tenants enjoyed a social life with sports, amateur dramatics and whist drives. Tenants were very proud of their village and the life it allowed them to enjoy, and today that pride and enjoyment are still there.

Garden Village, Burnage, c.1910 *(right)*

One of the aims of the Garden Village movement was to foster a community spirit, and here is evidence of success. Most of the "villagers" appear to be taking an interest in the proceedings of the annual Sports Day. Sports Days are still held showing that the community spirit desired by the founders continues to this day.

Burnage High School, bomb damage 29th November, 1940 *(below)*

Although the Fairey aircraft works were on the Burnage border, there was apparently no attempt by the German Air Force to destroy them. The only known record of wartime bombing in Levenshulme or Burnage is of the stick of small bombs which fell across Green End and Burnage High School. The late Mr. A. J. K. Swannell, a teacher of German there, had been telling the boys from 1934 onwards that war was looming again. He was right, and his school was an early victim.

Green End, 1888 (Drawing by S. B. Corbet)

The signpost points the way from Manchester to Didsbury, and the scene is Green End on Burnage Lane. Mauldeth Road stretches away up the hill. At the top of the hill on the left would be the gates of Mauldeth Hall, from 1847 to 1869 the Palace of the Bishop of Manchester. The estate was originally called Lee Gate (no connection with the Bishop, James Prince Lee) and the original house was said to have been built by the keeper of the Longsight Toll Gate. On the right is the lane to Hurst Farm, the buildings of which are visible to the left of the finger post.

Aerial View of Green End Road in the mid 1930's *(opposite)*

This view shows the cinema (The Lido), later the Burnage Odeon, and now the Concorde cinema and entertainment centre, and the Kwik Save supermarket. The tram tracks are readily visible on Kingsway, and there is a gap between the houses and shops on the left which has subsequently been filled. It is an interesting view of the layout of this large council estate which was built in the late 1920's, and which totally changed the face of Burnage. The playground and part of Burnage High School (opened 1932) are at the top left-hand corner.

Milton Cottage, Burnage Lane, c.1903 *(left)*

Milton Cottage (now a pub called The Sun in September) is on Burnage Lane about 250 yds north of Lane End Road, and was probably built about 1860 as a pair of very large semi-detached houses. 19th century maps show only farmland here before the houses, so that it is interesting to read the message on the postcard from which the picture is taken. It says "Paradise Found was written in the room the window of which overlooks the Lake". Perhaps it is a reference to the condition of Burnage at the time. The lake was drained in the 1970's and filled with hard-core, after which houses were built on the part of the site between the filled-in lake and the road.

Lane End, Burnage, c.1906 *(above)*

This is the heart of Burnage. There were scattered dwellings along Burnage Lane between here and Levenshulme early in the 19th century, but at Lane End there were already more than 30 old cottages, similar to those in the foreground, none of which remain. The shadowy building in the background is the Bull Inn (now the Old Bull Inn) partly hidden by the gable end of Burnage Post Office and the adjoining house which were built about 1870. The lane at the right of the picture led to a group of about seven old cottages, and from there by field paths to Pytha (Pithy) Fold, and on to Cotton Lane, Withington. Cotton Lane and Cotton Fields probably refer to the cotton grass, which is a wild plant of damp moorland. The gas lamp is the 19th century type, fluted-cylindrical, which was replaced early this century by a type with a more decorated base.

Except for the Old Bull Inn, all the buildings in the picture have gone, and only the pillar box on the pavement remains as a reminder of the old post office.

Burnage Post Office, Lane End, late 1890's *(top left)*

This was the corner shop of Burnage village, and probably a shop from the outset, judging from the amount of wear on the stone step. George Lowe proclaimed himself to be a provision dealer, and was licensed to sell Ale and Porter (a dark brown bitter beer brewed from charred or browned malt) to be drunk off the premises. His window also shows a collection of bottles containing either sweets or herbal remedies. The Post Office and adjacent buildings have been demolished and replaced by shops.

Burnage Band, Burnage Lane, c.1905

The scene is of Burnage Lane at Fog Lane, looking towards Parrs Wood, and the occasion is the annual procession of Burnage Wesleyan Methodists as they set off. The building on the left is their Mission Hall, opposite the end of Fog Lane. The Hall was demolished when the Hans Renold works were built in 1909.

Fog Lane, c.1910 *(left)*

This is Lane End – the Burnage end of Fog Lane. The terrace of nine old cottages includes one occupied by "M. L. Haskell, High Class Boot Repairer".

On Burnage Lane, part of the Hans Renold works can be seen, and, on the right, the Bull Inn (now the Old Bull). The village smithy is reputed to have been on the corner of Fog Lane and Burnage Lane adjoining the Bull, and this may account for the cutaway corner of the Inn. During the 19th century the smithy was rebuilt on the left-hand corner of Fog Lane, and pulled down when the road was widened. Before the widening the smith built a new smithy and cottage on the site behind the people seen here, but it is said that this was never used as a smithy, and it was eventually occupied by the Wesleyan Methodist congregation as a Mission Hall. The Hall site was acquired by Hans Renold as part of the land on which the new factory (seen here) was built, and the Wesleyans built another chapel farther along Burnage Lane, at the corner of Berwick Avenue.